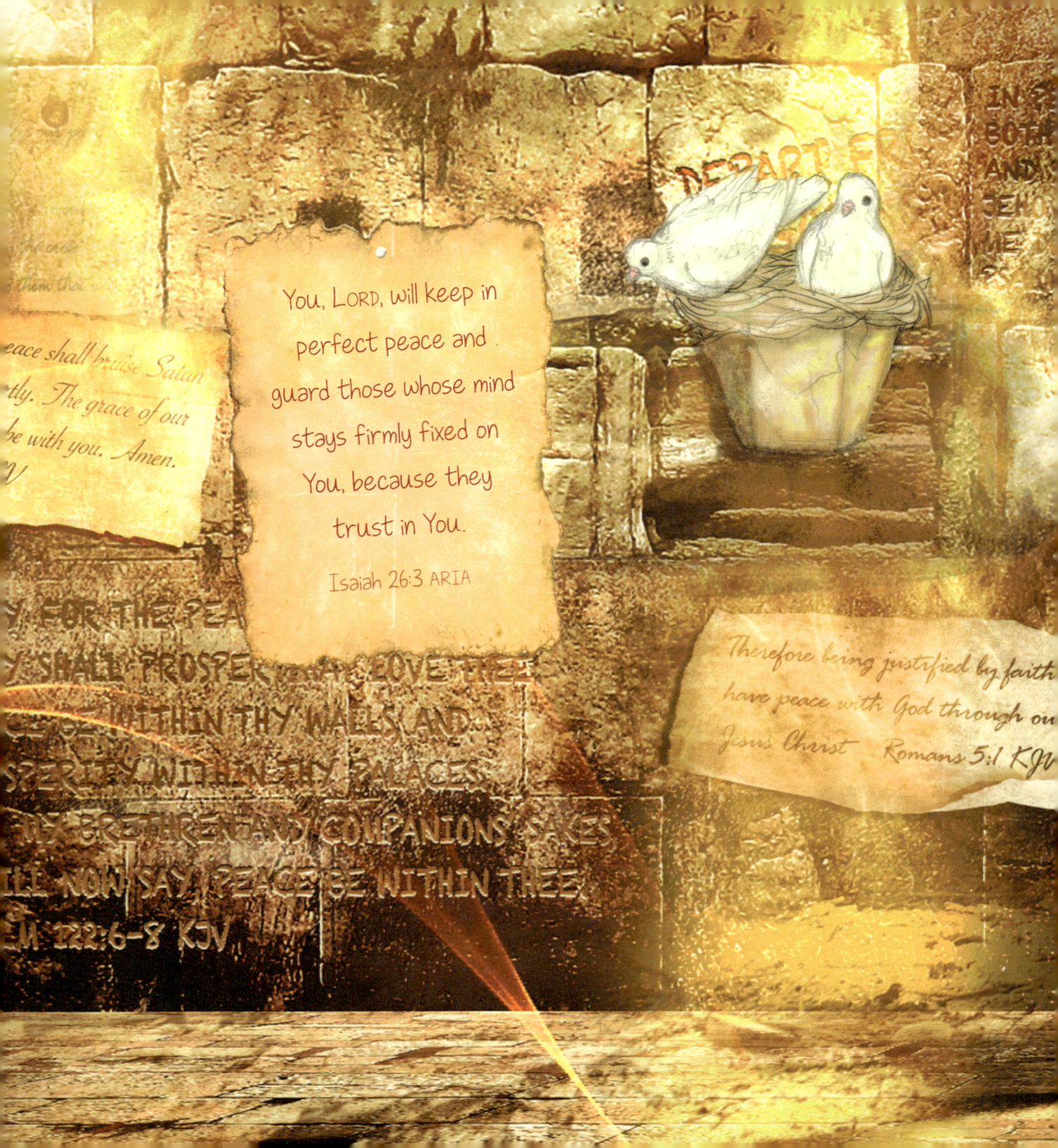

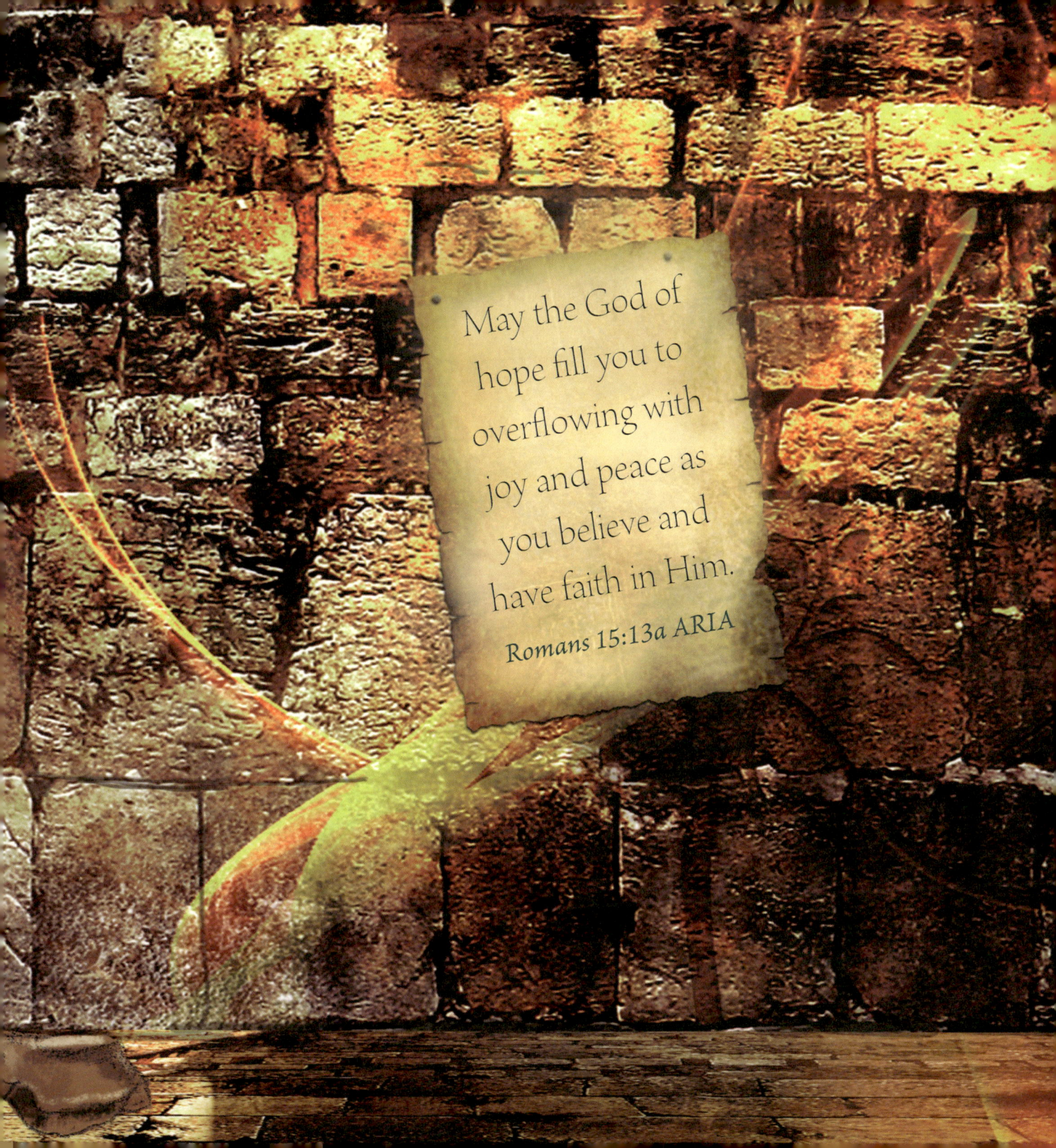

A Prayer for Peace

Thank you Heavenly Father for Your peace that You
give to us that comforts and surpasses understanding.

Thank you for giving us Your Word, the Bible, to hold onto in times of
trouble. That we can hope in You to protect us when seasons of life
seem dark, and yet Your peace remains with us. Thank you for Your
promises of restoration and that You welcome us into Your wonderful
healing light.

We pray that Your Word will continue to enlighten
and encourage us about Your love and peace that
You have for Your precious children.

Thank you Lord, that You are our ultimate Saviour,
who rescues us during hard times, and brings
comfort, joy and peace to our hearts.

Amen.

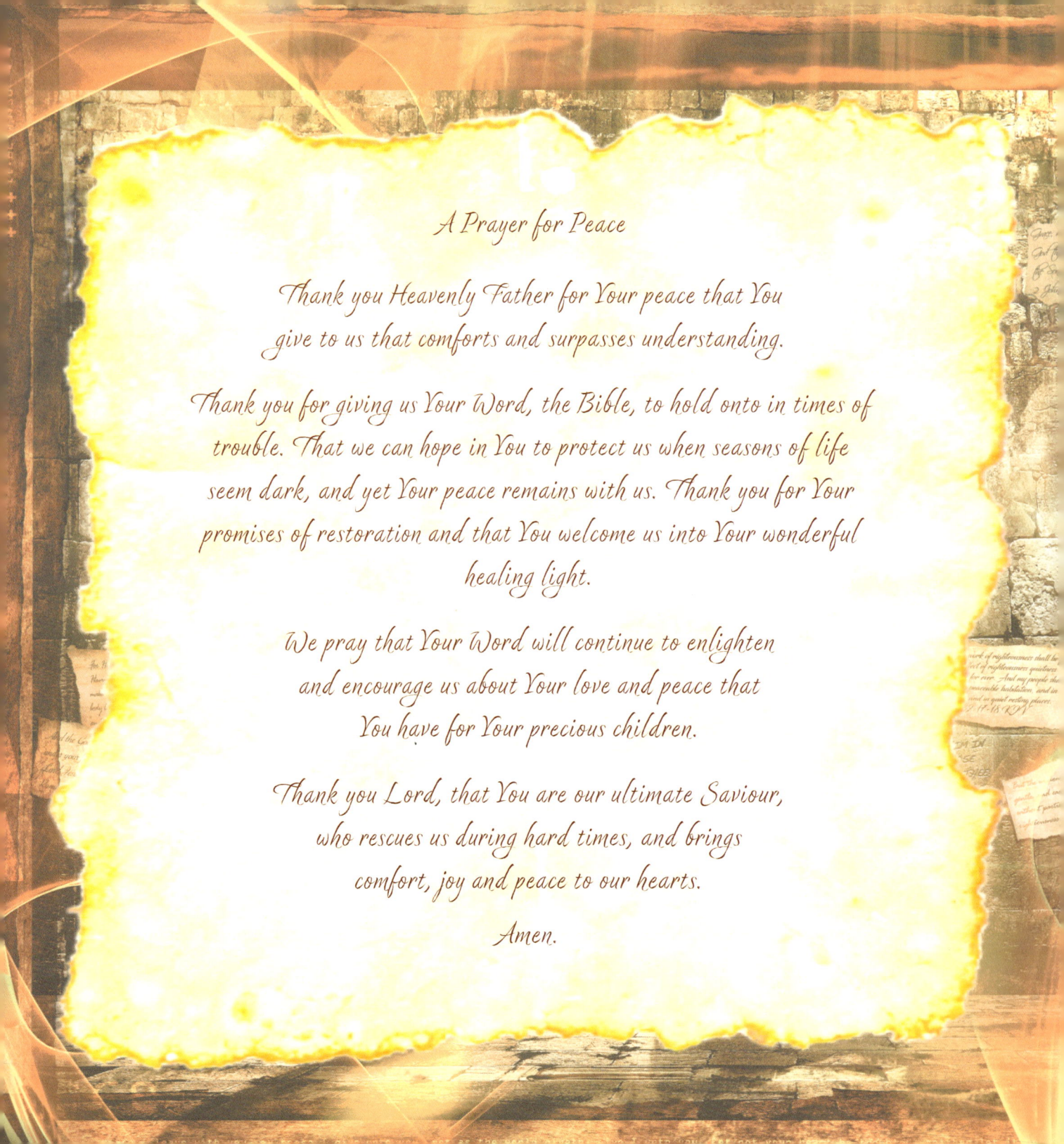

PEACE WALL SCRIPTURE ART

First published in 2021
by Dawnlight Publishing
This edition published in 2024
ISBN 978-1-99-117699-8 (hardcover)
ISBN 978-1-99-117683-7 (paperback)

Peace Wall artwork designed by Mike Burrows Graphics.
Book layout and illustrations by Mary Marinan.
Text, artwork and creative book concept copyright © Dawnlight Publishing 2023.

Scripture quotations from the King James Version and American Standard Version ~ public domain use.
Scpripture quotations from the Artistic Revived and Inspired Adaptation (paraphrase) ~ copyright © 2023 by Dawnlight Publishing. Used by permission. All rights reserved.

A catalogue record for this book is available from the National Library of New Zealand

All rights reserved. No part of this publication may be reproduced, stored in a retrieval system, or transmitted, in any form or by any means, electronic, mechanical, photocopying, recording or otherwise, without the prior written permission of the publisher. The only exception is brief quotations for the purpose of printed reviews.

Scripture Art Books

Scripture art coffee-table style hardcover books

Smaller paperback size

Writeable Scripture Art Books with space to write your own verses and prayers

Other titles by Dawnlight Publishing

Books, and books and journals in-one

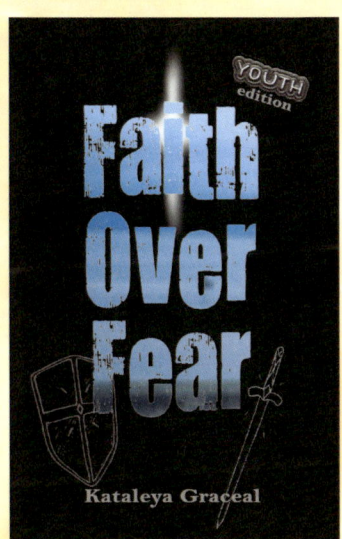

Poetry

www.ingramcontent.com/pod-product-compliance
Lightning Source LLC
Chambersburg PA
CBRC091208010526
44107CB00022B/1261